A PINCH OF
ROSEMARY

COUNTRY TALES OF LUST AND PASSION

CAROL PAYNE

FOREWORD BY

Keith Floyd

B🌿XTREE

This book is dedicated to my dear old Mum, Nellie May,
who inspired me to write it.

Contents

FOREWORD

Meeting Carol Payne for the first time is an amazing experience. From under the rain-dripping trees of her garden she sails out long black hair flowing in the wind, wrapped in long silks and satins like the female lead of an eighteenth-century Spanish opera.

Sail she does like a galleon under full sail scattering a flotilla of duck and geese before her.

She starts to talk from about a hundred feet away. Speaking fast like a Gatling machine-gun. Except she's firing philosophy, wit and love instead of bullets.

She tells tales of rumbustious naughtiness of yesteryear. Soft tales of country folk. Told with passion and an appealing sexuality.

She cooks pigeon and lentils in a big brown pot. That smiles at you. She sweeps through rooms perfumed by exotic flowers. That slash colours over you. Like rainbows from a silver bucket.

She paints with bold rich sensuous colours. You want to eat or make love to the pictures. They are naughty. They are funny. They out-shine the sun.

They are the embodiment of what life, love and food should be about.

Carol Payne achieves this in spades.

Keith Floyd

INTRODUCTION

This book is all about the 'Naughty Goings On' that took place mostly in the countryside and generally from the earlier part of this century. The stories of Lust and Passion are all based on truth and sexually, saucily and romantically reflect my paintings. This was a time when many a maid lost her virginity in a haystack or old barn, and when a glimpse of white starched petticoat and black stockings exposing a neat ankle was enough to 'stir up' a man's most 'private parts' and set his heart beating at a great pace. Food, Love, and Music were the essential ingredients of life, and to 'air one's dirty linen in public' was a disgrace.

I had gathered these stories for years mainly from the old folk, (many who have since died but now their memories could linger on forever) who would relate them with a twinkle in their eye. The tales were often humorous, usually scandalous but never malicious. Many came from my mother whose father worked for the Lord of the Manor in Dorset. I had never dreamt of making them into a book by linking them to my paintings. However, one day my old mum was looking at one of my paintings for ages, her eyes lit up as she recalled in great detail a story about a young maid she knew who worked in one of the old manor houses. The Lord was a 'dirty old devil' and . . . well, if you read *A Pinch of Rosemary* you will find out what happened.

THE BIRDS BEGAN TO SING
The Saucy Sea Captain's Secret

Pinkie was an attractive middle-aged woman and the wife of a wealthy Lord who was a 'Dirty old Devil'. She knew all about her husband's indiscretions with the servants and the young maids in the village, so she took to having crazy parties with banquets of delicious foods. The parties kept her busy, providing her with a means of having fun and compensating for her husband's lack of love. Music would accompany the orgies of food and there would be lots of singing, drinking, dancing and love-making.

Pinkie kept white fantail doves as a hobby, although it was considered vulgar for a woman in her position to do so. One summer's evening when she had just finished feeding them, she saw her husband talking to a dark-looking stranger with a big black bushy beard, and a strong confident voice. He was a sea captain and when he introduced himself by kissing her hand and impertinently gazing into her eyes at the same time, Pinkie was immediately attracted to him. His eyes were as brown as conkers and framed with thick black lashes, and she wasted no time in inviting him to one of her banquets.

She would get the cook to bake a magnificent pie and fill it with a dozen young doves trained by her to sit on her head and dance on her fingertips. This would surely impress the sea captain. On the night of the party Pinkie looked exquisite and so did the pie, which was carried into the big hall by six bare-chested muscular servants, who were wearing white turbans on their heads. The pie was richly gilded and decorated with bunches of green grapes, glazed carrots, nuts and bay leaves. The sea captain was indeed impressed and his mouth opened at such a splendid sight. He leant up close to Pinkie whispering obscenities, words of passion, what he would do to her when they were alone, and she felt his strong fingers under the starched white table cloth searching for her thighs. She knew the night was hers.

Well it was, until the choir of several black ladies sang 'Oh for the wings of the wings of a Dove' and Pinkie flicked the lid off the pie with a knife. The young white doves flew out of the pie and landed on her head. Triumphant with her efforts she looked around at her sea captain, but he had gone red and stiff, then fainted and disappeared in an undignified heap under the table. Neither smelling salts nor a splash of cold water revived him. The last Pinkie saw of her sea captain was him being carried out by four servants, and he never returned.

Pinkie eventually discovered that the sea captain had a phobia about all sorts of birds, dead or alive. They put the fear of God into him, and the phobia could be traced back to a nasty childhood experience. He had been tormented and terrified when he was a little boy by a bullying father who had made him witness and help in the slaughtering of poultry.

SHE THOUGHT THE ELABORATE PIE WOULD MAKE HIS EYES SPARKLE.

TITBIT

The making of elaborate pies goes back to the Middle Ages, when pies could contain all manner of unusual things, such as squirrels, foxes, frogs, snakes, blackbirds (hence the nursery rhyme *Sing a Song of Sixpence*) and even live midgets. Medieval dovecots were a means of supplying fresh meat all the year round. The squabs are the very young doves still being fed by both their parents with pigeon milk, they are sweet and juicy to eat and therefore used in many old recipes.

SUSAN WAS A SECRETARY
The Ring Master's Mistress

Susan was a good old-fashioned prim and proper secretary. She worked in a large Victorian manor house in the Buckinghamshire countryside for an antiques dealer. For ten years she sat behind her typewriter tapping away, dressed in a conventional knee-length grey skirt and a white shirt with a string of pearls around her neck. She tied her long blonde hair up severely in a bun.

She was quite content with life. She owned a picturesque thatched cottage with roses growing up the walls, and she had a steady boyfriend. When she woke up in the morning she knew exactly what the day would bring. Well she thought she did.

One day, when she was out in her garden gathering loads of windfall apples, a young man came riding past on a magnificent white horse. Susan couldn't take her blue eyes off him. At first he didn't notice Susan gaping at him but then suddenly she let out a great yell—a wasp had just stuck its red hot sting into her thigh.

The young man pulled his horse up an asked if she was alright. It was at this moment that their eyes met and Susan felt her stomach turn over as his dark brown eyes gazed right into her soul. Susan fell in love with the man on the white horse and they became lovers. She discovered that he was a ring master with his own old-fashioned, traditional circus.

It was not long after this meeting that Susan's life changed dramatically. She left her job as a secretary, sold her pretty thatched cottage and started a new life with her ring master. Prim and proper Susan had joined the circus, and soon she had her own act in the sawdust ring. Off came her grey conventional skirt and her white shirt, to be replaced by a leopard skin—it was a very revealing, figure-hugging garment. Her long blonde hair was allowed to flow around her shoulders and her pearls were replaced by a massive python that entwined itself around her curvaceous body.

Susan loved the circus life, and performing with her pythons; but her greatest performance was reserved for the evening when everyone had gone home. Her ring master would appear in the sawdust ring, naked, except for his top hat, white gloves and a circus whip. He would flick and crack the whip around Susan's leopard skin cloth until it dropped off on to the ground. Then the two of them would roll around in the sawdust for ages making mad passionate love.

Susan had indeed become the ring master's mistress.

SUSAN WOULD INVITE THE AUDIENCE TO STROKE HER PYTHONS.

PEACE ON EARTH
Doreen and her Brassicas

*D*oreen looked as though butter wouldn't melt in her mouth. Even when she stood at her easel, painting cabbages in her father's vegetable garden, she always looked beautiful and elegant. Her waist-length blonde hair was tied up neatly behind her shoulders in a scarf, and her delicate long white fingers were always carefully manicured, and often painted with scarlet nail varnish. She was the perfect English rose.

One day, as Doreen stood knee-deep amongst the rows of cabbages painting a cowpoll (a massive cabbage with silvery green veins which is fed to cattle), a swarthy young man, with black wavy hair and vivid blue eyes, appeared behind her, causing her to drop her paintbrush into the cabbages. Doreen recognized him as the gypsy who had recently appeared in the village. She stood for a moment staring him straight in the eyes; she was nervous of the dark stranger who had entered her vegetable garden without being invited.

Ignoring her he bent down and tenderly fingered the leaves of the cabbages with his fingers. It was then that Doreen noticed that on one of his fingers he wore a massive gold keeper ring with a diamond in the centre. As he fingered and fiddled with the cabbage leaves she felt herself staring at the back of his neck, his hair was black and shiny and his neck was strong. A cabbage white butterfly settled on his head. She had an uncontrollable urge to blow the delicate insect away, and as she bent forward to do so he stood up abruptly. He was by no means handsome, but his eyes were an extraordinary borage blue, and they looked wild and exciting.

Doreen finished painting and she felt strangely anxious as she saw him disappear through the old painted door of the walled vegetable garden. She pulled the big savoy cabbage that minutes earlier the gypsy had been fingering and went indoors with it under her arm. She couldn't get him out of her mind. As she put the cabbage on the scrubbed pine table in the kitchen something dropped out and clinked on to the slate floor. It was the gypsy's gold ring.

That night she couldn't get the gypsy out of her mind. She tossed and turned all night, dreaming that she lay naked with him in the savoy cabbages, her white skin in complete contrast to his and the knobbly dark green leaves of the cabbage. He read her palm, gently stroking it with his long strong fingers, kissing her all over. She woke up in a hot sweat disappointed to find it was only a dream, then she remembered his ring and she decided to return it to him.

The next day she went to the field where she had seen his gaudy painted caravan and sure enough there he was, stripped to the waist in the cold morning sunshine, washing himself in a chipped enamel bowl. She felt again her stomach flip over as she gazed at his strong body. But she also felt extremely nervous and she was just going to leave when he looked up and caught her gaze—she felt her cheeks go red. He bid her 'good morning' and invited her into his caravan.

It was amazing inside the gypsy's caravan—everywhere Doreen looked there

DOREEN DREAMT SHE LAY IN THE BRASSICAS WITH HER GYPSY LOVER.

were things of interest and it smelt pleasantly of tobacco and lavender. A pair of fantail doves were in a cage in the window billing and cooing and preening their feathers. Cushions in faded red velvet with gold tassels were tossed on an unmade bed, horse brasses were everywhere, coloured china crowded a dresser which was painted with white doves and red poppies and bedecked with bunches of herbs.

When she had finished looking around the gypsy gave her a glass of nettle beer and he sat close to her, still naked to the waist. Doreen couldn't get her eyes off him and she felt a tingling sensation all over her body. What an exciting challenge he was! She felt mesmerized by his vivid blue eyes as he stared at her and she flirted with them unashamedly.

From that day on Doreen spent as much time as she could with the gypsy. She was greedy to learn his ways! Although he was uneducated he knew more about nature than any of her farmer friends and in his company she was never bored. He taught her where and when to gather herbs and their uses and all about animals and their ways. He showed her how to make wine from wild fruits and berries and, in his gaudy painted caravan on the faded red cushions, he made love to her uninhibitedly and passionately, like she had never been loved before.

In the summer months he decorated her hair with elderflower blossoms and would then take her deep into the heart of the secluded woods behind his caravan. There he would make love to her amongst the ferns, where the greedy midges fought and argued over her naked white body. Then later, using his strong fingers, gently he would massage an elderflower cream into her bites, kissing her passionately all over as the cream eased her discomfort.

Inevitably her parents became suspicious, especially when she returned home smelling of lavender and tobacco and her breath smelt of garlic. One day, when the autumn leaves were falling from the trees, Doreen went to his caravan. But all that remained of her love nest was a smoking bonfire, smashed beer bottles and a broken clay pipe. Frantically she searched in the woods where they used to go and she found his shirt all torn and covered with blood and next to it lay one of his white doves, dead.

Doreen never did see her gypsy lover again. But that night, as she prepared to go to bed, a white dove flew through her bedroom window and roosted on top of her wardrobe. It stayed with her for twenty-two years until it died.

TITBIT

The elderflower cream that Doreen's gypsy lover massaged tenderly into her white delicate body is easy to make and is an excellent healing and soothing cream for heat bumps, bites and chapped hands.

Put 1lb (450g) of pure vaseline (or pure lard) into a saucepan, with as many elderflowers as possible (remove the stalks). Allow to simmer for about three quarters of an hour. While still hot strain through a sieve or a piece of muslin into pots. Use when cold.

Brassicas are descendants of the wild sea cabbage which still grows around the white cliffs of Dover. The word cabbage comes from the Latin *caput*, meaning head. The brassica family includes Brussels sprouts, cauliflower, broccoli, spring greens, kale and all the other types of cabbage. It is a very underrated vegetable as it contains many important minerals and vitamins.

Two words of warning: never overcook cabbage for the vitamins and minerals will be destroyed; and if you are planning a night of lust and passion avoid healthy cabbage because it can cause great flatulence.

THE PHEASANT PLUCKER
The Gamekeeper's Mistress

*E*ddy Barnes was a fine young gamekeeper with a cheeky look in his eye who worked for the Lord of the Manor. The Lord was an old rogue but an excellent employer, considerate and kind to his men. At Christmas time all his workers were given a brace of pheasants, a leg of pork and a party was held in the old tithe barn, which would be decorated with holly and ivy. All the workers and their families would attend and there would be much singing and dancing to a local band. People worked hard, but times were good, and they understood their purpose in life.

As gamekeeper, Eddy took care of the breeding of quails, pheasants and partridges. On his twenty-first birthday the Lord of the Manor gave him a beautiful white baby ferret for his good work and as another means of catching rabbits. The young gamekeeper was delighted with his gift. He called the ferret 'Chew' (the old name for a ferret is 'fitchew') and he kept it in an old hessian sack attached to his belt. The young ferret was tame and playful and never left the gamekeeper's side.

The Lord of the Manor had several children. One was wild, beautiful, with long black hair, and blue eyes. Often, when her father was away, she used to sneak out of the house and watch the young gamekeeper feeding the pheasants; when Eddy saw her watching him (being a Lord's daughter she never spoke to him) he used to

THE YOUNG PHEASANT HAS FIRM PLUMP BREASTS, AND SHINY PLUMAGE.

show off. He would take his ferret out of the sack and play with it, gently fondling the creature. Her eyes lit up when she saw him caressing the ferret.

One day the Lord of the Manor appeared on a magnificent bay horse, looking very impressive in his hunting outfit. The Lord enjoyed hunting but there was no sign of his wild daughter, as she hated to see the fox being killed. Minutes later the Lord's daughter appeared, wearing a long brown velvet dress, a bunch of blue flowers in her hair and a straw hat perched on the back of her head. She gave the gamekeeper a long twinkling wicked look and then disappeared into the old barn where the pheasants were hung. The young gamekeeper stood gaping at the door, not daring to move. Presently she poked her head around the barn door and beckoned to him with her finger. Without hesitating Eddy followed her into the barn, glancing nervously over his shoulders as he did so, making sure no-one was watching.

The Lord's wicked wild daughter lay in the hay, her white cat lay nearby purring loudly. Her dress was unbuttoned down to her waist, exposing her milk-white body. A great wave of passion and lust swept through the young gamekeeper's body as he gazed upon her, and his ferret fidgeted around in the sack tied to his waist. He felt the soft velvet of her dress, and then the silky texture of her skin. He kissed her and she responded so passionately. The young gamekeeper suddenly felt anxious; if he was caught in the barn with the Lord's daughter he knew the consequences: he would be sacked, lose his tied cottage and be banished from the village. Sensing his fear she said, 'Don't worry, father's gone hunting and he won't be back for ages and ages, and he always ends up having a drink with his friends.' Her voice was clear, soft and very inviting and reassuring. Eddy put his arm around her, kissing her face, her neck, her lips, her body—he was over-whelmed with passion. Suddenly he felt his ferret stirring. The girl's eyes sparkled at the sight of the splendid wriggling creature, and she stroked it rather timidly at first. Eddy gently took it from her and popped it back into the sack. Then he untied the sack from his belt and placed it next to him. He looked at her again. Never before had he seen anything so beautiful and he kissed her once more on her warm sensuous mouth.

Suddenly, there was a terrific banging and the door of the barn was pushed open and a terrified fox shot past them and ran out of a broken window. 'Oh no, it's father,' the Lord's daughter shouted, jumping up and quickly buttoning up her dress. The young gamekeeper leapt behind the hay bales, but forgot the sack

containing the ferret. She quickly grabbed the sack and popped it under her long velvet skirts amongst her petticoats.

The Lord of the Manor appeared on his horse, riding it through the barn door; the horse was snorting and sweating with all the excitement of the hunt. The Lord was so surprised to see his daughter there, but before he could question her she shouted: 'Quickly father, the fox, it went out of the window a minute ago,' and he galloped off with his dogs barking behind him.

As soon as the Lord rode out of sight the gamekeeper appeared looking very worried, but broke into a cheeky grin when she showed him where she had hidden his ferret. 'I wish I had hidden there with him,' he said, and gave her a great passionate kiss. He then grabbed the sack containing the ferret, tied it to his belt, and was about to leave when she said, 'I must see you again.' In the distance they could hear dogs and horses—her father was returning. The young gamekeeper ran out of the barn. 'Tomorrow then,' she shouted after him. But he was gone.

TITBIT

The pheasant is a beautiful bird and the younger it is the more tender the flesh and its breasts are firm and plump. Buy the bird 'undressed' not plucked then you can see how young it is by its shiny plumage. A pheasant must be hung for at least six days to have the flavour of the wild still in it, otherwise it will be dry, tough and tasteless.

To cook the pheasant a good stuffing inside is essential and will help keep the bird moist. A generous knob of butter, zest of an orange or lemon and fresh garlic will do nicely. Lay strips of bacon across the breast and baste it with the surrounding juices of honey and sunflower oil and cook it slowly and gently.

When the pheasant is nicely basted, cooked and browned it is traditional to decorate it with the beautiful tail feathers, and garnishing it with bunches of fresh watercress and green grapes.

SCARLET RUNNERS
The Market Gardener's Mistress

Prim and proper Winnie Pinch was the apple of her husband's eye, he worshipped the ground she walked on. She was a proud plump attractive woman, well respected in the village, with a mass of red bushy hair, greeny-blue eyes and a rather large bossy nose and lots of gingery freckles all over her body. Winnie was also fastidious and fanatical about everything she did.

But then one sunny September day, when the church was packed out for the Harvest Festival celebrations, Winnie shocked them all. She appeared in church looking stunning and different, wearing the most fantastic emerald-green satin dress. It had layers and layers of buttercup-yellow rustling petticoats underneath (frou-frou petticoats, as they were called, were very fashionable in the early 1900s). As she walked up the aisle she rustled them as loudly as she could by wiggling her hips to and fro, while the old organist played 'All good gifts around us'. On her head she wore an enormous straw hat that was covered with carnations, runner bean flowers, satin bows and a net veil hanging down over her eyes. Prim and proper old-fashioned Winnie Pinch caused a sensation.

It was an old Raleigh bicycle that Winnie's husband had given her that changed Winnie's life so dramatically. She was cycling through the countryside one day when she came upon a sign saying 'Runner Beans For Sale', and it was here that she met Freddy Forster the market gardener. Winnie found Fred in the potting shed with his shirt off and she couldn't take her eyes off his muscular chest. Fred had fallen out with his wife and he too was attracted to Winnie. They had a drink or two of Fred's blackberry wine and afterwards Winnie cycled home feeling a bit squiffy, very strange and light-headed.

They did meet again and again and Winnie had a passionate love affair with Freddy on his raised bed of potato sacks in the old potting shed, amongst the spiders and beetles. Winnie was obsessed with him. No longer did the absence of spotless starched sheets worry her. Winnie had never experienced passion like this before.

Sadly the happy pair were found out a year later when the runner beans were ready again for picking. Miss Tonkin, an old miserable spinster, was walking her dog near Fred's allotment when it ran off barking into the rows of the scarlet runners. There Miss Tonkin found Winnie in the arms of Freddy Forster, who was kissing her passionately on her 'gingery freckles'.

Prim and proper Winnie's love affair had come to a sad and abrupt end.

WINNIE PINCH WAS HAVING AN AFFAIR ON FRED'S RAISED BED.

CORN DOLLY
Cuddling in the Corn

iana was nicknamed Dolly because when she was about a year old she looked just like a china doll, with her big dark-brown eyes, long black curly eyelashes, turned up snubby nose and a mass of black curly hair.

Dolly was born in a small village in Dorset and had four sisters, Cybil, Mona, Olga, and Beatrice and two brothers, Norman and John. Dolly was a different kettle of fish than her other sisters, who were rather old fashioned and straight-laced. She was a tall, striking looking young woman, an excellent swimmer and tennis player and as strong as an ox. She also had a keen interest in boys. In fact she started kissing boys behind sheds, in barns and lying with them in haystacks and cornfields when she was fourteen years old. Yes, Dolly King had had several passionate love affairs before she was married and she was considered by many women in the village to be a loose woman—a 'meadow lady'. She jilted one young man and he was so distressed he threw himself down the village well after a night of heavy drinking and was killed instantly.

Her father was a miller and owned his own baker's shop where all the daughters helped out; he also owned two magnificent sheep dogs called Ben and Bonny. The two dogs followed Dolly everywhere and they also used to catch the rats which ran around in her father's mill. Being as strong as an ox her father insisted she help in his fields, haymaking and reaping the corn. This was the perfect time for everyone to have a gossip, a chatter and a flirt with the men and, maybe, sing a song or two. Although it was hard work Dolly enjoyed working in the fields, whilst her other sisters stayed at home cooking and sewing. It gave her the freedom to flirt and the opportunity for much kissing and cuddling in the hay ricks. It was whilst she was working in the fields during haymaking that Dolly fell in love with Albert. He was one of the 'Baker boys'—a family of ten, tough muscular young men, who used to help Dolly's father with the haymaking and any other jobs that needed strong healthy young lads. Dolly loved to watch their muscular brown bodies, tossing the sheaves of corn up on to the cart and throwing the hay on to the ricks. Yes Dolly was well and truly in love with Albert Baker; he was twenty-three years old and Dolly was nineteen. In June 1927, on Dolly's twenty-first birth-

DOLLY LOVED KISSING AND CUDDLING IN THE HAYSTACKS.

day, they were married and Dolly settled down to married life. The couple lived in a tiny cottage built of Portland stone, near to her mother and father's baker's shop.

After fourteen years of marriage the Second World War broke out, Dolly was thirty-four years old and there was still no sign of a baby, so she was considered barren. Unfortunately, Dolly's husband was called up. Suddenly the village was alive and buzzing with gum-chewing Americans, who handed out chocolates, cigarettes and nylons. The women buzzed around them like bees around a hive.

It was at this time that Dolly started to behave in a very strange way. She started swimming in the dangerous mill stream, sometimes completely naked. The local people thought Dolly had gone a bit odd because she couldn't have any children and she was missing her Albert.

There was one big American called Red because of his mass of gingery red hair. He was an officer in the United States Air Force and he was always popping in and out of the baker's shop, noticeably when Dolly was helping out there.

One moonlit warm wet evening Fred Tucker was sitting quietly on the river bank near the mill, minding his own business, enjoying the peace and quiet while fishing for trout. He saw Dolly through the bulrushes, floating on her back in the moonlight completely naked, her large breasts bobbling about on top of the water like a couple of floats. Suddenly from underneath the water like King Neptune emerged a naked Red, lifting a screeching Dolly high in the air in his arms, his ginger hair and Dolly's white body a striking contrast against the murky muddy water in the moonlight.

Dolly's two sheep dogs were nervously pacing up and down the water's edge, whining, watching them and guarding their clothes. Red took Dolly in his arms thrusting his robust body against hers, pushing her head backwards nearly into the water, kissing her neck and body passionately. The both stayed in this position for ages, bodies locked tightly together, rhythmically bobbing up and down in the dark moonlit mill stream. They could have stayed quite happily there all night but Fred Tucker, the nosey old devil, leant forward just a bit too much and slipped into the river. Ben and Bonny suddenly started to bark. Dolly and Red scrambled quickly out of the water and both sheep dogs greeted them, licking their faces, relieved to see them safely back on shore.

Eventually Red went back to America and Dolly's husband returned from the war. Within a short time of Albert returning Dolly announced that she was pregnant—and so did three other 'barren' women in the village.

Dolly's baby girl was born a month premature. She weighed only five pounds but had a mass of black hair. They called her Queenie. Dolly was relieved when she saw the baby's black hair—just like her parents'—but when the baby was about two years old her hair gradually changed to a deep rusty-red gingery colour. This turn of events was ignored, for Queenie was such a beautiful baby and she brought great happiness to Dolly and her husband. Dolly was a different person. She was contented and happy and a year later she announced that she was pregnant again.

TITBIT

A corn dolly was part of the pagan tradition. It was cut from a large sheath of corn collected at harvest time, then made into a shape of a woman and decorated with garlands of ribbons and given different names. It also helped to protect the family from evil spirits in the winter and was planted out again the following spring, to bring them good luck and another good harvest.

Lady in Red
A Bear Lover

Queenie grew up to be a smashing looking girl, a bit wild like her mother, a lover of life and men—particularly the Americans. She had a mass of red curly hair down to her waist, green eyes and white skin like porcelain.

Queenie met her American at the American Air Force base dance. His name was Richard but his friends called him 'Big Dick', because he was very tall. Dick wore lots of Old Spice aftershave and spoke with a southern drawl. He had a

QUEENIE'S RED LIPSTICK MADE HER MOUTH LOOK WARM AND SENSUOUS.

strange lop-sided grin that showed off the most amazing set of gleaming white teeth Queenie had ever seen. They were greatly attracted to each other and they spent the evening eating popcorn, drinking vodka and gin and dancing cheek to cheek.

It was the middle of October and the trees were showing their autumn hues. Leaves fell withered from their branches like confetti. She and Dick were going by train to London Zoo. Queenie felt really excited and she looked stunning. They both kicked happily, like young children, at the rustling red autumn leaves as they walked hand in hand together through the zoo. Dick looked very dashing in his American Air Force uniform, with his little hat perched on the side of his head. His dazzling smile and the smell of his Old Spice aftershave made Queenie's heart pound with excitement. She was proud to be with her American.

Presently they came across a large crowd of people leaning over a wall pointing and laughing. 'Come on let's go and see what they are looking at Honey,' said Dick. But before they continued any further he stopped under a huge weeping willow tree and kissed her passionately. Queenie liked Americans because they were so affectionate and uninhibited, and they always made a great fuss of their women. Queenie's grandmother used to say that Americans were overfed, overpaid and oversexed and that's exactly why Queenie loved them.

The weeping willow trailed over Queenie's face. Dick pushed the branches away from her cheeks, took her hands in his and put them around his waist pulling himself close to her, pressing his body hard against hers. Queenie kissed his lips passionately. Dick had such a generous, kind mouth and his teeth were so white and perfect. She just loved kissing his warm sensuous mouth.

Then Dick grabbed Queenie's hand and ran towards the crowd, pushing his way through. He leant cockily over the wall to see what everyone was laughing at and they found themselves looking straight into a bear pit. Two enormous brown bears were pacing up and down, it was near to feeding time and they were very agitated. Dick started showing off, like all young men, and leant even further over the wall into the bear pit, grinning widely at the bears. In the excitement his hat fell off into the bear pit. Dick let out a yell. When he turned around and faced Queenie he was as red as a beetroot. Queenie was stunned because he was now toothless! He was just gums, those gleaming white teeth had gone! They both looked down into the bear pit and there was the biggest brown bear licking Dick's teeth while the other bear chewed his hat.

The keeper rescued Dick's teeth but everyone had shared the joke at Dick's expense. All the way home toothless Dick didn't utter a word, or smile. He was still feeling very upset and embarrassed. Queenie didn't say much either. Every time she thought of the bears with his teeth she started to laugh. She felt very sorry for Dick because he had lost his lovely teeth, his hat, his confidence; but worst of all 'Big Dick' had lost that lovely sensuous smile. Fickle Queenie never felt the same way for her big American again.

DAMSON TART
The Mistress and her Servant

my Cudmore was possessed of a ruthless desire to better herself. She came from a poor Cornish farming family, so poor that Amy was made to wear underwear made out of flour sacks which were printed with red, bold letters 'THE FINEST FLOUR'. Life was very tough for Amy. Her father was an old tyrant and a drunk and she was made to work hard in the home, looking after all her brothers and sisters and doing the housework. The only relief from this dreadful life was her music and her great love of the countryside.

Amy left home at fifteen to become a scullery maid. She earned a shilling a week

AMY HAD AN UNCONTROLLABLE URGE TO REMOVE HER COMPLICATED CORSET.

to put in her pocket, and another which she sent home to her mother. At twenty-two her strong Cornish accent had disappeared and she had grown into a graceful young woman. It was her elegant appearance and neat figure that got her the important job as a parlour maid in an isolated mansion in Devon.

Amy looked stunning in her very close fitting black woollen dress with tight long sleeves and a white muslin apron with matching collar and cuffs. On her black shiny hair she perched a white cambric cap with a frill. The owner of the house, an earl, a tall distinguished old gentleman with a long curly moustache, took a shine to Amy. Soon she was doing him all sorts of little 'favours' to keep him happy—and it wasn't just grooming his moustache!

Several years later, by her own cunning and patience, Amy Cudmore became mistress of the house when the old countess died. At first life was wonderful. Amy learnt how to play the violin and she spent hours in the library studying nature books and entertaining her husband's guests. The old manor house improved with a younger spirit in charge. She also managed to persuade her husband to employ several male servants of her choice. Although it was very fashionable at this time to wear lingerie, Amy became obsessive about it—perhaps understandable after wearing flour sacks for years. Her corsets were so intricate in design and so complicated, it took half an hour for her maid to lace them up. The earl had enjoyed doing this for Amy but had become so old and infirm that he was confined to a wheelchair and couldn't do anything 'active' anymore, so he relied totally on his servants.

It was not long before Amy had become frustrated and lonely. She started walking through the fields and woods and taking picnics down by the river on the estate. One hot summer's day, having eaten her picnic and consumed the best part of a bottle of damson wine, she had an uncontrollable urge to remove her clothing and have a swim. Without hesitating she lay back on the grass and whipped off her clothing, but when she got to her batiste corset she couldn't undo it. Flustered and cross she continued twisting and turning the corset, grinding her teeth in the most unladylike manner when a voice called out, 'May I help you madam?'

Amy was so embarrassed but very slowly she turned around and, her heart thumping loudly, she perceived a very attractive young man, much younger than herself. It was her husband's valet. Calmly and cooly composing herself, but looking into his eyes and flirting with them mischievously, she said, 'Well as you help the master undress you might as well help the mistress.' Without any hesitation, the young valet took care of his mistress, unlacing her corsets gently and slowly, his nimble confident fingers knew exactly what to do. Amy was beside herself with excitement, she found the whole experience so pleasurable.

The two of them built up a wonderful relationship and the young valet stayed in her 'service' for a very long time. Amy Cudmore never struggled with her corsets again!

TITBIT

In the early 1900s the batiste corset was a very fashionable and indeed an essential garment for all elegant women. It was constructed of very intricate panels of satin and lace and reinforced with whalebones and steel busks in the front and laced up the back. Once the corset was on it was a very restricting and uncomfortable garment to wear, especially in hot weather. It was also necessary for someone to help remove the corset, but this could be a marvellous prelude to love making. Perhaps this is why it was so popular! The manufacturers said it improved your health and endowed your form with charming and attractive qualities.

DAMSON WINE

Damson wine is very similar to port, and although it takes ages to pick all the damsons it's well worth the effort. Care must be taken that the fruit is ripe, sound and unbroken. In a year the wine may be bottled and after two years the flavour is much improved and it brings a wonderful sparkle to the eyes.

THE PRIZE COW
The Fruity Farmer's Fondles

Samuel Devlin was a large stocky man with an appetite like a horse. He sported a bristly ginger beard, had massive strong hands and beady brown eyes with a hint of mischief. He was the head cowman on a big estate in Dorset and he took great pleasure and pride in taking care of his cows and bulls. Samuel also took great pleasure in chasing the milkmaids round the milking parlour—he couldn't keep his big chunky hands off them. All the new milkmaids working there were warned about Mr Devlin.

His wife was a small plump middle-aged woman, with a constant nervous sniffy twitch. They had six children and unfortunately after every birth she went a bit peculiar. You could tell when she was about to enter this odd phase because she made a strange clicking sound with her tongue. She knew all about Samuel's flirting and fondling with the milkmaids, but chose to ignore it.

One day, shortly after giving birth, she was cooking casserolled cows' udders in a thick white onion sauce, when Samuel returned home from work. He was starving hungry and whistling happily with a big smile on his face—and smelling strongly of a sickly sweet perfume. He had just had a cuddle and a nibble of Doris the milkmaid's big breasts. But his big smile soon turned to anger as his wife, sniffing and twitching, slopped the greasy cows' udders on his plate. He shouted angrily at her for serving up what 'poor folk in the Union get'. At that moment his wife's tongue started to click and the blood pounded round her face. She screamed and screeched hysterically as she picked the udders up with her bare hands and slapped him aggressively around the head and face with them. The hot slimy sauce ran down Samuel's red cheeks as she chased him out of the house and down the lane, smacking him with the udders, still shouting and swearing.

Not long after this mildly amusing event Samuel was leading his prize bull by a strong chain which was attached to a brass ring in the bull's nose. It had been raining and the old cobblestones in the courtyard were slippery. Samuel slipped and fell, pulling extremely hard on the ring through the bull's nose as he went down. The bull became very angry and gored Samuel to death while he lay on the ground. After Samuel's death his poor wife went really mad and she and the children were sent to the Union—a place of rescue for the poor and needy.

SAMUEL HAD A PASSION FOR MILKMAIDS.

TITBIT

Almost every part of the farm animal was cooked and eaten in the old days. Popular recipes included fricasseed cow's feet, cow's head with parsley sauce, sheep's feet with bay leaves, pig's trotters in cider, dried pig's cheeks, calf's foot jelly, bullock's heart with herb stuffing, fried ox feet and stewed ox tails, and tripe and onions—even the pig's ears were not wasted. Cows' udders, however, was a poor man's dish, the udders being very rubbery and tough to eat. Samuel's wife probably served them up deliberately as was her cussed way.

Peaches and Dreams
The Sunday School Mistress

The brass band played loudly on the sweeping lawns of the old Georgian vicarage. Men, women and children were laughing and chattering, dancing and singing, and the vicar and his wife were talking to the old people.

A group of little girls, who were waiting to take their turn at folk dancing, sat at a trestle-table near the azaleas with Charity, their young Sunday School mistress. Charity looked as 'pretty as a picture' sitting there at the table in her pink dress and her hat full of flowers. But she looked so sad, and when the male voice sang 'One man went to mow, went to mow a meadow' and 'Green grow the rushes O', everyone joined in the chorus except for Charity.

She rose from the table and walked towards the corner of the garden, rustling her dress past the vicar who didn't even acknowledge her, to where the morris men were dancing. Then she heard: 'Under the yew yew tree, you and me, a tickling me', and couldn't believe it. Only the night before in the churchyard, she had met 'him' under the old yew tree. Had he really caressed her last night, enveloping her in his long black cloak or had she dreamt it?

Charity couldn't stand it any more. The vicar was still ignoring her so she went past him once more. He still didn't acknowledge her. Suddenly she had had enough so she went up to him and interrupted his conversation. 'Oh Father I think I have left my purse in the church and I am just going to see if I can find it.'

She rushed off to the church hoping he may follow her. Her plan worked out and ten minutes later she heard the big oak door opening. 'I can't find my purse anywhere Father,' she said coyly. He didn't look at her at all but darted in and out of the pews searching for Charity's purse. 'Oh don't worry now Father, I have found it,' said Charity.

He turned around and she stood boldly in front of him with her skirts gathered up high, around her waist, exposing her satin pink petticoats and white silk stockings—she wore no 'other' undergarments—and the little silk purse was tucked into the top of her stocking secured by a pink satin garter. The vicar gasped at such a sight and gazed at her splendid long legs and he felt the blood pounding around his body and he saw a look of passion in her eyes, and once more like the previous night he felt the devil stirring in his trousers.

Suddenly Mrs Potter, the church warden, came in the church calling the vicar. She stopped when she saw the two of them together. 'I'm sorry Father if I disturbed 'ee, but the children are going to dance now, and you told me to come and get you.'

He went quickly towards the door, sweeping the floor with his long black habit, brushing away petals that had fallen from the flower displays. Just as he got to the door he stopped for a moment and gazed at Charity a long-lasting and lustfull gaze, and then he was gone.

HAD SHE DREAMT THAT HE HAD CARESSED HER LAST NIGHT?

A. Bird Lover
A Cornish Crumpet

When I was a child my old mum used to invite to our home several waifs and strays, sad lonely people who had nowhere else to go, to share our lovely Sunday roast dinners (considering there were nine of us in the family it was very kind of her) and afternoon teas of salmon and cucumber sandwiches, trifle, fruit cake and victoria sponges. Amongst them was little old orphan Annie, who was about five feet tall, with grey hair and a pudding-basin haircut. Poor old Jack the hunchback who hadn't a tooth in his head, Paddy an Irish man who lived on a houseboat on the canal (when the canal iced over he rescued two swans and they now lived on the boat with him) and old Arthur the dustman.

Now Arthur used to entertain us by playing the mouth organ and bringing gifts, which were objects that he had rescued and repaired from the dustbins. Arthur was a clever fellow with a great sense of humour and he was a good story-teller. He used to make my mother laugh by telling her amusing stories that he had seen or heard whilst collecting the dustbins. One such story is told of Cocky Robbins.

Cocky Robbins was probably Jewish or perhaps Hungarian. He was an odd character, quite old, in his late sixties with a bald head, biggish nose with hairy nostrils. He had a rather large mole on the side of his face that had a black whisker growing from it, and a mouthful of gold fillings. He owned a pet shop in town and was supposed to be worth a 'bob or two'.

Although he kept all sorts of animals, he was first and foremost a bird lover and he specialized in parrots, amazons, macaws, parakeets and cockatoos. Cocky Robbins used to buy the parrots direct from a dealer as small chicks and hand rear them. The parrots became very tame and he could then sell them in his pet shop for a lot of money. Cocky used to strut around the shop with a huge blue and yellow macaw on his shoulder. His obsession with birds was supposed to be the reason why Cocky Robbins acquired his nickname but Arthur wasn't convinced. Cocky Robbins had been married three times before and had outlived all his wives. He was a mean old devil and although he was supposed to be rich he never

COCKY ROBBINS PREFERRED TO REAR HIS OWN BIRDS.

employed anyone to help him in his shop and he always looked miserable and hardly ever smiled, except at his parrots.

One day much to everyone's surprise there was an unusual-looking woman working in the pet shop. She was in her thirties and wore tight skirts, red shiny high-heeled shoes, fish-net black seamed stockings and very tight gaudy jumpers that showed off her large bouncy bosoms. She also wore lots of black eye make-up and red glossy lipstick. Her hair was black and shiny and she often wore it up, inside a large red beret. Arthur said her red lips were always tight and puckered like a 'chicken's arse' and he thought that she believed that she was on to a good thing, meaning she wanted to get her hands on Cocky's money! She had a strange accent and she said she had come from Mevagissey, a small fishing village in Cornwall. She looked a cross between a tart and one of Cocky Robbins' parrots and Cocky was immediately attracted to her. She told him she was an out of work actress and had worked as a trapeze artist in a circus.

Cocky fancied this Cornish Crumpet (Arthur's word for her) and Arthur said that old Cocky Robbins had definitely perked up since this 'bird' had arrived. She also seemed to have an effect on his parrots. The big blue macaw on his shoulder screeched even more and Cyril's (the cockatoo) crest was always bobbing up and down excitedly. The mynah bird added even more words to its remarkable vocabulary. Cocky even painted the shop, something he hadn't done in years, and he added even more pets to his collection. Business was booming and he even started to smile, showing his gold fillings. Sometimes the smell of home-made pasties and Cornish splits wafted out into the pet shop and into the back yard where Arthur collected the dustbins.

One sunny Wednesday afternoon, when the shop was closed, Arthur went to collect the dustbins from the little concrete yard at the back of the shop. Arthur said that you could tell there was a 'bird about', because even the yard had changed. The dreary old yard was suddenly alive with colour. There were tubs filled with geraniums, snap dragons and pink petunias. A clothes-line hung across the yard and Arthur stopped for a moment and stared in amazement at the rows of 'fluttering frillies' that brushed the top of his cap; the silkiness of the nylon flirted cheekily with his face. He felt the frilly garments with his hand, holding them close to his cheek, trying to imagine the Cornish Crumpet in her underwear. Suddenly from within the house he heard the blue macaw let out a terrifying screech and Arthur thought he heard the mynah bird saying, 'Oh Cocky, Oh Cocky, naughty boy, stop tickling!' and then it panted, sighed and giggled realistically. There were no lights on in the house and Arthur couldn't resist taking a peek through the old net curtains to see what all the noise was about. There, much to his surprise, lying amongst the large sacks of sunflower seeds and dog biscuits, was Cocky Robbins and beside him the 'Cornish Crumpet' almost naked except for her large red beret, red gloves and red patent shoes. She was giggling and screeching and pursing those puckered lips at him; the old cockatoo's crest was going up and down and Cocky Robbins had a grin on his face like a Cheshire cat. The big blue macaw went on screeching. You could say that Cocky Robbins was feathering his nest and the Cornish Crumpet wasn't objecting—after all she was on to a good thing!

$\mathscr{P}$ICNIC IN $\mathscr{M}$AY
Naughty Nellie

$\mathscr{N}$ellie May had already been out with George's older brother Douglas but George was much better looking, although he always looked so sad and hardly ever smiled. Ivy, George's sister, had told Nellie that George didn't like girls very much and he was feeling very down and depressed. Their father had a drink problem and his liver was packing up so they sent him into hospital to try and sort him out. George was very close to his father and the last thing George wanted to worry about or even think about was girls.

Anyway, during one of the cricket dances on a Saturday night in the village hall, Nellie, chaperoned by her brother Fred and accompanied by Ivy, met the tall dark, good-looking George.

GEORGE'S EYES LIT UP WHEN HE LOOKED AT NELLIE'S TASTY TITBITS.

The Cricket Blues Band was playing that evening; it was Nellie and Ivy's favourite band. They both had a marvellous time doing all the latest dances. At every opportunity Nellie would give George the glad eye, and at one time she spun around so fast she bumped into poor George, who was having a quiet drink with Fred. Eventually, George took the hint and asked Nellie to dance. George's wide, grey-flannel Oxford bags nearly touched the ground and they wrapped and flapped themselves around Nellie's legs as they danced cheek to cheek. Ivy's comments about George not liking girls were definitely wrong. Once George had Nellie in his arms, he didn't want to let her go, especially when they danced the stately waltz. He held her so close and tight that Nellie could feel every muscle in his body, and she did the whole dance virtually on tip toe.

It was a wet warm June evening and George decided to walk Nellie home after the dance. He was feeling light-headed and happier than he had felt for ages. Following close behind George and Nellie were Fred and Ivy. They all took a short cut through the dark cemetery. Nellie didn't enjoy walking through the churchyard, it was always full of adders in the summertime, but tonight she was in for a pleasant suprise because dotted everywhere amongst the long grass, even on top of the tombstones, were the sparkling flourescent lights of glow-worms. George took several of the glow-worms and stuck them in the brim of his hat, and they made their way to Nellie's cottage with his hat glowing in the dark.

When Nellie went to bed that night she couldn't sleep. She lay thinking of handsome George, and although she was cross with him for teasing her, she rather liked the way he had admired her legs. She couldn't wait to see him again. She even planned in her mind to go and buy another pair of saucy garters from Wimborne.

After that night the affair blossomed; George and Nellie used to meet at every opportunity. They played tennis, went to church together, and there was dancing twice a week, often accompanied by Fred and Ivy. In fact they were so happy and in love a wedding was planned for May the following year.

It was May Day and a week before the wedding of Nellie May and George and they were going for a picnic down by the river. George had borrowed Nellie's father's fishing rod which he stuck in the river bank, and he carried a wicker picnic hamper containing all sorts of tasty tit bits that Nellie May had carefully prepared.

Nellie spread the spotless white table-cloth on the grass and sat down. George's eyes lit up as he looked at Nellie's tasty tit bits. There was salmon sandwiches, quiches, quail's eggs, strawberry tarts, love cake, rum truffles, savoury pies, chocolate cakes and a bottle of home-made parsnip wine.

George was feeling good after drinking the parsnip wine. He lay back resting his head on May's lap, nestling his head comfortably between her small firm breasts, delighting in the delicate apple blossom perfume she always wore to please him. 'Have you got your garters on Nell?' whispered George, turning over to face her. He ran his hand under her dress searching for them. Nellie May tingled when she felt George's fingers on her thigh, playing with her garter.

'I can't wait to marry you George,' Nellie said, leaning over him, holding his head and kissing his forehead. Her gentle gloved hands felt like butterflies on his face. Their lips met and he could hear her heart beating loudly and he noticed the pupils of her eyes dilating, covering nearly all the blue of her blue, blue eyes. Nellie felt sick with happiness and love, so sick, she couldn't eat a thing. She loved and wanted him so much that she nearly wept with passion and happiness.

Suddenly his rod started to move about, thrusting backwards and forwards and bending into the water, he shot up and pulled a fine rainbow trout from the river. 'George it's too beautiful to kill, please let it go, throw it back into the river,' pleaded Nellie May, looking at the poor writhing fish. George looked at May's sweet face, the sadness in her eyes, and he gently took the big gleaming trout off the hook and carefully threw it back into the river.

'My darling dearest Nellie May, you are also too beautiful to eat, but I'm not going to let you go,' said George, engaging himself gently between May's legs, causing her flimsy dress to rise up higher and higher, exposing both green satin garters. Her stomach turned over at these words and they lay like this for ages cuddling, touching, kissing passionately and murmuring sweet nothings to each other.

Nellie and George were not married in May like they had hoped. George's father died suddenly, so the wedding was postponed until Boxing Day that year. In December 1926, in the little old church of St Peter's in Hinton St Mary, Dorset, Nellie May married George Hodges.

NELLIE MAY HAD A LOT TO CELEBRATE. SHE HAD FALLEN IN LOVE WITH GEORGE HODGES ON MIDSUMMERS' NIGHT.

$\mathscr{M}$ISS $\mathscr{C}$OQ-AU-VIN
The Poultry Keeper's Bird

There was in Buckinghamshire a poultry farmer called Hedley. He used to be in the navy and had tattoos on his arms and all over his body, mostly of eagles and other birds, but on his left leg he had a tattoo of a naked woman holding a cockerel. Hedley's knowledge of chickens and ducks was remarkable—he was one of the few chicken sexers in England. Chicks can only be sexed within a few hours of hatching; sometimes Hedley found himself being called out in the middle of the night to sex chickens all over the country.

Hedley kept thousands of chickens in a big stone barn. Next to the barn was a large wooden building. This was a plucking shed, where the freshly killed chickens were subjected to an automatic chicken plucker. Nearby was a smaller barn completely covered in ivy. It was here that the eggs were stored and graded. Sometimes Hedley would grade his eggs to the sound of loud opera. Singing very noisily and out of tune, his hair standing on end as if he had been electrocuted.

One day a nice 'free-range young hen', with firm plump breasts, came to work at the poultry farm. By coincidence her name was Vanessa Cock. Vanessa was a punk rocker and it was quite astonishing how much she resembled a chicken, with her mass of red stiff-lacquered hair and long pointed fine nose.

Hedley found himself attracted to this odd, well-spoken and obviously intelligent 'bird' and it didn't take long before he took Vanessa under his wing and was soon teaching her a thing or two about chickens. Vanessa was very keen to learn.

Hedley told her that in the old days they used to use a capon gun to desex the cockerels but, much to his distaste, most chicken farmers now inject the young cockerel with female hormones. Although Hedley had a plucking machine, he told Vanessa it was important to learn how to pluck by hand. It didn't take Vanessa long to become an experienced plucker of all sorts of poultry.

Vanessa and Hedley spent hours in the plucking shed together, with the door firmly shut, plucking happily away to the sound of Mozart's *Figaro*. Vanessa cuddled up to Hedley like an 'old hen' when they roost at night cuddled up to the cock. Vanessa's bright red hair spiked and lacquered stood up even more, just like a hen's comb when she is fertile and laying.

Then an odd thing happened, Vanessa started to change her style of dress. First the black leather jacket and her tight jeans were replaced with more conventional clothing. Her hair, which was obviously dyed red, returned to its natural brown. She stopped lacquering it, so it didn't stand up on end.

Hedley's taste in music changed too. Instead of opera, love songs could be heard drifting from the plucking shed. He began to comb his hair, he shaved his beard off and started bathing and showering every night; he changed his socks every day and began wearing an expensive after-shave. His wife wasn't very happy about the situation and she started to get extremely jealous. Hedley was spending

VANESSA SOON BECAME AN EXPERIENCED PLUCKER.

more time in that plucking shed than he did in the house and 'feathers started to fly'. Eventually Miss Van Cock, the poor girl, was sent packing.

Vanessa moved to Wales and started her own poultry farm with free-range hens, quails and Aylesbury ducks. She dyed her hair red again and lacquered it, began to wear black clothes once more and added several more gold ear-rings to her ears. She would encourage her hens to lay all through the winter by feeding them cooked potato peelings and by keeping their feet warm. Instead of opera and love songs the sound of heavy rock music echoed over the Welsh valleys from her record player in the plucking shed.

Titbit

There is a very old story that says when a cockerel roosts at night he 'rules the roost' by always roosting next to the fattest and youngest hen. This is the hen you should choose to eat, because it is supposed to be tender and juicy with nice firm plump breasts. Charlie, my old cockerel, who suffers with bumble foot (he's the cockerel in the painting) sleeps every night in the middle of his five fat hens. In the winter they completely enclose him with their warm feathers. I think he's just a crafty old cock myself.

*L*ADY IN *W*AITING
Lusting Lily of the Valley

*G*eorgie Bone was Cornish and a Methodist preacher. Not only did he put the fear of God into his congregation but he also ruled his own home with fire and brimstone. His two daughters, Lily and Grace, were terrified of his rantings and ravings and his loud booming voice. The girls and their mother lived in poverty and in fear of him. At meal times, the girls sat like mice at the table whilst their father spread his bread with butter, allowing the girls the last salty rancid scrapings from the barrel. Everyone was frightened of Georgie Bone, even their old dog hid under the stairs when he returned home after a morning of preaching.

Both girls couldn't wait to leave home and get married. Unfortunately their chances of meeting a nice young man were pretty slim because their father wouldn't let them out alone. Their mother, although a kind little woman, was in her late forties and had recently become deranged as a result of the 'change of life'. Any

THE VICAR TWITCHED NERVOUSLY AS HE GAZED AT LILY'S BEAUTIFUL BODY.

young man who had the courage to enter the house was in for a shock. Mother would sit with both feet plunged into a bowl of water, staring and swearing like a trooper at them and occasionally spitting in their direction.

Despite their strange parents, the two sisters grew into very interesting, if somewhat unusual, girls, and they were both very pretty. Even the village people were amazed by their beauty.

Lily had long wiry, thick wavy ginger hair, skin like white porcelain sprinkled with freckles and a rather attractive mole in the centre of her forehead. She was eccentric, outspoken and smoked a clay pipe. In the summer, when the sun shone brightly, Lily would take her pipe and stand naked in the centre of a clump of bamboo at the bottom of the garden, puffing happily away. Eyes shut, her chin and firm small breasts thrust upwards towards the heavens, she looked like a statue.

Lily was 'a hard-working loyal and trusting girl'. The vicar was old enough to be Lily's father, but Lily found him very attractive in an odd sort of way. She adored his beautiful English-speaking voice, his soft unworked hands, with carefully manicured finger nails and his immaculate clothing. She had never seen a man like this before. When she discovered he came from a very wealthy aristocratic family, she worked out a plan 'to get' the vicar by seducing him.

The vicar's matriarch of a mother lived with him. She frightened the life out of the servants and any women who tried to cross the Reverend's threshold. Lily hated the way the mother dominated her son but was not frightened of the old woman.

The old matriarch was partially deaf and as bald as a coot; she wore a wig to conceal her bald head. On Thursday mornings the old lady had both her wigs shampooed and set, and she never got up until they were returned to her, which was late in the morning. So Lily decided that a Thursday morning was the time to pounce.

She rose as usual at six o'clock, put the big kettle on the old range, and prepared the vicar's tray. The vicar liked things hot and she wasn't going to disappoint him this morning. She looked at herself in the ornate gold mirror that hung in the hall. 'Lily my flower you look good this morning,' she thought to herself as she stood for a few moments studying her looks and figure in the looking glass. She then removed her cap and pins from her hair and allowed her long shiny ginger hair to cascade around her shoulders.

Promptly at seven o'clock she knocked on the vicar's bedroom door. Presently he answered 'come in'; she gave him a few more minutes allowing him time to put his false teeth in and then she entered the room. The vicar still had his back turned

to her whilst she poured out his tea. This gave Lily the opportunity quickly to slip off her clothing; she hadn't put much on this morning, no undergarments, just her black stockings held up by garters. In seconds her dress and apron quietly slipped to the floor, on to his old leather slippers that were next to the bed. She bent down, desperately trying to pull off her black stockings when she noticed that the garters were too tight and had left an horrendous ugly red mark on the top of her legs.

He turned round to face her and he couldn't believe his eyes. Lily was totally naked except for her black thick stockings. Her white porcelain body glowed in the darkness of his room and her ginger hair trailed over her freckled shoulders. The vicar twitched nervously and vigorously rubbed his eyes—he had never seen a young woman like this, so pure and beautiful. Not for one moment did he think she was the 'maid from downstairs' more like a 'messenger from heaven'. His prayers had been answered and, before he had a chance to recover his senses, Lily cooly jumped into bed with him.

A year later, in the spring, Lily married the vicar even though her father and the vicar's mother were against it. The vicar took his new young wife to live in an old rambling vicarage in a lush green valley with a garden overgrown with azaleas and arum lilies, leaving the old matriarch to move in with another son.

RED CARNATIONS
Hello Mr Magpie

*H*er ladyship saluted Mr Magpie three times chanting out loudly, 'Hello Mr Magpie, Hello Mr Magpie, Hello Mr Magpie' as the large black and white bird flew past her bedroom window. She was going hunting today, and she didn't want any bad luck. Suddenly something caught the corner of her eye. Lady Katherine saw Rosie the kitchen maid running out of the coach house, buttoning up the front of her bodice and pinning up her hair as she ran.

Lady Katherine could not keep her thoughts to herself and shouted out aloud to Iris Crump, her loyal lady's maid of twenty years, who was patiently trying to brush Lady Katherine's hair: 'Something's up in that stable yard I know it is, I have seen Rosie going in and out of there every morning this week. Last week, too, I'm sure I saw the scullery maid dart in there.' Iris Crump replied that Bill, the head horseman, had a reputation for being a bit of a 'stallion' with the young 'fillies' of the area.

Lady Katherine pressed her face hard against the window-pane, kneeling one knee on the chintz window-seat. She could just glimpse Bill coming out of the stable now, leading a handsome seventeen-hand steel-grey 'teaser' stallion to a splendid chestnut mare. Lady Katherine pressed herself even harder against the cold wet window-pane and wondered what these 'fillies' saw in their 'stallion'. Iris Crump went on and on about Bill's sexual prowess in her broad Cornish accent until Lady Katherine could take no more. The thought of Bill, the head horseman, thrusting himself around with the 'fillies' made her feel fidgety and excited. Iris Crump, as if reading her Ladyship's thoughts and knowing how her Ladyship liked 'a bit on the side', said quickly, 'Mind ee I don't know if 'ee could handle a real Lady. 'Eee wouldn't know what to do.'

The sun was just beginning to shine through the fog and the huntsmen and women were assembling in the cobblestoned courtyard.Lady Katherine could hear people laughing, dogs barking and excited horses stamping their impatient hooves on the frozen leaves as she walked to the yard to mount her horse. Bill held the horse's head as she wriggled herself into position in the new side-saddle. She looked stunning in her emerald green velvet hunting outfit and she knew it! She wriggled her hips provocatively from side to side making the leather squeak, glancing at Bill's face as she did so.

Whilst everyone rode off she called to Bill to help her adjust the girth. Lady Katherine took her whip and flicked him hard on the shoulder, a deliberately strong flick. Bill stopped what he was doing and looked up at her. She held her whip in her hand and lifted the edge of her skirt high above the top of her riding boots, exposing her red flannel petticoats and matching red stockings. Bill feasted his eyes on her scarlet legs for a moment, thinking what to do next. 'The bottom of the ridge in five minutes,' Lady Katherine demanded in a cool icy voice. She rode

HER LADYSHIP WAS A FINE FILLY, JUST RIGHT FOR MOUNTING.

off, head held high, out of the yard into the countryside.

It didn't take him long to tack up his horse and make his way to the ridge; he knew a short cut to the secluded dip at the bottom of a steep ridge. Presently at the end of the long line of huntsmen Lady Katherine eventually appeared and skilfully rode her horse down the edge of the ridge, weaving her way in and out of the narrow track to where Bill stood waiting. Without hesitating Lady Katherine lifted her leg high above the pommel of her new side-saddle and almost fell into his arms. Bill caught her and held her firmly around her tiny waist, she was as tall as him but his grip around her waist was so strong. 'Damn it man,' she muttered in her elegant voice, 'take me like you would my kitchen maid. Quickly, quickly.' She flung herself against his firm body and Bill's hand felt her body was warm and inviting. He found his way quickly and aggressively among the froth of her red petticoats.

They stayed locked together against the trunk of an old tree until she could take no more. Lady Katherine stood up straight and adjusted her clothing by shaking her skirt and petticoats. Bill helped her back on to her horse, but he held her ankle tightly not wanting to let it go. She gave him a cool half smile and rode off, without giving him a second glance, to join the hunting party. She rode like the wind, she felt good, a new charge of energy within her. Iris Crump was wrong, she thought, he did know how to handle a lady.

Bill continued to 'serve' Lady Katherine for quite some time, but eventually he left to take charge of a large yard where they bred Arab horses.

Many years later, when Bill was an old man, but still with a twinkle in his eye, an elegant old lady brought her fine Arab mare to be served at the yard. Bill ran his hand over the mare's hind quarters and his fingertips gently down her legs, talking to the young mare in a soft caressing voice. 'What a beauty you are, just right for mounting.'

The old lady tapped him with a whip firmly on his shoulder and said in a voice as clear as crystal, 'I can remember Bill when you used to say that to me.'

Titbit

> A 'teaser' stallion is led to a mare which will squeal excitedly if she is ready for mounting. At that point the 'teaser' is led away and a well-bred stallion introduced.

ℱRESH ℬASIL
Buxom Bessie

B asil was feeling very pleased with himself. It was Boxing Day and he had been made Hunt King for the day. He looked a handsome sight with his faithfull old lurcher dog Lady at his side and dressed in his plus-fours, cap and leather gaiters. About forty men and the Lord of the Manor had gathered at the local Bell Inn, in preparation for the rabbit hunt. It was an old tradition that had gone on for 150 years, and Basil had been selected to be the Hunt King this Christmas because of his knowledge of the countryside.

He was the pest controller and employed by the Lord of the Manor on a big estate in Cornwall—his main job was to keep the rabbit population down, but he was often called upon to get rid of other pests such as rats, adders, moles, hornets' nests, squirrels, mice, and even caterpillars. Many of his customers were also 'naughty' ladies who required his 'services' when they were bored and lonely!

One such lady was Buxom Bessie. Basil had met her at the Hunt Supper, where she was helping out for the evening.

BASIL COULDN'T WAIT TO GET HIS HANDS ON BUXOM BESSIE.

[43]

After a tiring but exhilarating day, the men were all full of good spirits for they had bagged 120 rabbits, so it was back to the inn were they had begun the hunt for another old tradition, the Hunt Supper.

After an orgy of food that consisted of game pie, cold roast beef, ham and tongue, cheese, pickles and home-made bread, washed down with endless tankards of ale, Basil and the men were well and truly squiffy. Old yarns, dirty songs and several toasts were made and there were countless visits to the toilet, which was an old stable in a cobbled yard at the back of the inn. The 'old boys' were priviliged— they were allowed to use the pear tree near the pub.

It was on one of his frequent visits to the bathroom that Basil, on the way back, bumped into Buxom Bessie the serving wench. It was indeed a very pleasurable experience for Basil and it made him feel very fresh and fruity as he pressed his body firmly up against hers. Her long wiery blonde sheepy hair trailed over his face, and she smelt sweetly of rose-scented perfume.

She was delighted to bump into Basil and with a saucey, wicked look in her eye told him all about the trouble she was having with her squirrels—the little rascals were coming in the house and eating all her fruit and driving her mad. 'Comes and see's me in June while my husband is busy working in the fields, and then 'ee can sort my squirrels out,' she said to him, and then mischievously winking she added that she would give him a nice big glass of her clover wine, that was guaranteed to bring a sparkle to his lovely dark brown eyes! Basil responded to her offer by wiggling his body to and thro against hers and squeezing her big breasts firmly. He would be delighted to sort her little rascals out!

Spring came quickly and it was soon June. A pigeon sat on the roof of Basil's cottage preening its feathers, and several housemartins quickly collected the pigeons' plucked feathers in their beaks as they floated in the air, to line their nests. Meanwhile Basil was inside his cottage preening himself; it was a lovely day and he was off to sort Buxom Bessie's squirrels out.

Basil took his bag, containing an evil-smelling liquid in a green bottle that the squirrels and foxes hated. Lady, his dog, came with him while he made his way to Bessie's cottage, passing her husband in the fields turning the hay. As they crossed a green cornfield dotted with red poppies a young hare jumped out right in front of them. Basil whistled gently and the leveret stood up on its hind legs mesmerized.

A flick from his finger and Lady had the hare by its neck and killed it instantly. Basil tied the hare's legs together and slung it over his shoulder, and whistling happily made his way towards Bessie's little slate cottage.

The cottage was overgrown with old-fashioned marigolds and purple lupins, with roses and a sweet-scented honeysuckle over the front door. What amazed Basil was that everywhere he looked, there were squirrels. They were in the vegetable garden eating the strawberries, underneath the rhubarb leaves, sitting with the chickens perched on the roof. Basil then looked up and there was Bessie, her huge breasts resting on the bedroom windowsill above his head. She was delighted to see him and beckoned to Basil to join her upstairs, and she would show him where the squirrels were getting into the house.

Bessie wasted no time as she poured Basil a glass of wine, and as she handed it to him she thrust her body against his with so much pressure his cap fell off and nearly sent him flying. He dropped the old canvas bag that held his smelly fluid, and drank the wine greedily. She continued to rub her netted breasts on his chest, wiggling her body suggestively, she then removed the rose from her dress and stuck it in his hair.

Basil could take no more. The blood pounded around his body and his heart beat at a great pace. He pounced on her like a tiger, flinging her on the brass bed which rattled under such sudden weight. He pulled open the front of Bessie's dress—he had never in his life seen such a splendid pair of bosoms as these before and he greeted them like two long lost friends by holding them in his hands and kissing them both passionately.

Basil's face was red and hot as he set about Buxom Bessie who didn't stop him. Neither of them were aware of the two little faces watching them from the skylight

above their heads. Now whether it was the sight of the nuts in the bowl, the strawberries in the dish, or Bessie squealing that attracted the squirrels, but one large squirrel hurled itself on to Basil's back and the other one jumped in the nut bowl.

Basil lept up in the air as the squirrel's claws dug into his back and like a demented demon, his passion well and truly nipped in the bud, he shook the creature off. The squirrels ran for their lives through the skylight as he ranted and raved and swore like a trooper. He grabbed his smelly rag from his bag, dipped it into the evil-smelling solution, and rubbed it everywhere, even over Bessie.

He ran out of the cottage grabbing his leveret as he went, his dog following him. Basil was like a raging bull as he ploughed back through cornfields, over hedges, through gates, still swearing and cursing when he bumped smack into Bessie's husband returning for his lunch. He asked Basil if he had managed to get rid of the squirrels. Basil replied that he had and gave Bessie's husband the hare—to help ease his conscience. Basil thought he had succeeded in bluffing things out but then Bessie's husband called out to Basil. 'Oh by the way Basil, I like that flower in your 'air.' Basil went bright red and never said a word. He had forgotten about the damned rose that Bessie had stuck in his hair. He had also forgotten the cap he had left in Bessie's bedroom.

You could say that the 'squirrel was out of the bag'.

TITBIT

Fresh basil is the king of herbs whose flavour increases with cooking. It originates from India but it has grown in this country since the sixteenth century, but it does like a nice hot bed to grow well. In its dried powdered form it was once used as snuff and also as a love token.

RHUBARB TART
The Choir Master's Mistresses

arold Hancock was not only the choir master in a little village in Dorset, he was also a dirty old devil. He was tall and thin, dark skinned with an ugly wrinkly old face and was married to a little mousey lady who bore him twenty-two children, of which sixteen survived. He was an accomplished musician and played the cornet in church. He also played the organ with great skill! Harold just couldn't leave the women alone.

SHE LOVED RHUBARB BUT SHE LOVED HER CHOIRMASTER EVEN MORE.

It was a great joke amongst the village boys that old Hancock's flies were always popping open, especially if he had to play the organ when the women's choir was singing. In fact the village boys used to follow Harold Hancock whenever they noticed him leaving his cottage. One day they saw him enter Bessie Scott's house whilst her husband was out working. Freddy Whitlock was fifteen years old and a cheeky young lad, and he and his gang were waiting behind Bessie's stone wall when Harold Hancock arrived at the house. They gave the choir master fifteen minutes inside Bessie's pretty Portland stone cottage, and then Freddy climbed the stone steps leading to the front door. He banged on the cottage door, shouting and hollering. Presently the window upstairs opened and a very red-faced Bessie flung a full chamber pot out of the window over Freddy's head.

After this affair there was Winnie Parrot, another middle-aged woman. She had frizzy light brown hair and pale blue eyes, and she was a real dunce when she was at school. But whatever Winnie lacked in brains she compensated for with her cooking skills. She was rather old fashioned and she still wore comfortable long skirts and black woollen stockings; her hair was pinned up in a cottage loaf style. Winnie was married to an old cobbler and they had five children. Winnie owned a pony called Dapper that she harnessed up to a small nursery cart. She used this pony and cart to collect the large bundles of rhubarb and other produce that grew on her husband's allotment.

By coincidence the plot of ground where the old cobbler grew his vegetables was next to the choir master's allotment. The two men even shared the same large old wooden shed. They divided the old shed down the centre with a wooden partition and each shed had its own small window and a door for access. The old cobbler painted his door red and the choir master painted his pea green.

Now Minnie used to pay several visits to that old shed, usually just after lunch whilst her husband was busy at work. Strangely enough, at the same time old Hancock would go into his side of the shed and after about half an hour Winnie would appear looking rather flushed; five minutes later Harold Hancock appeared with his flies popping open.

One day Winnie came flying out of the red door screaming loudly and seeing Freddy and his gang standing there gawping at her, exclaimed that there was a big spider in the corner of the shed and could one of them remove it. Freddy, without hesitating, volunteered. It was very dark inside the shed and there was an odd damp, musty smell. Winnie pointed to a massive fat-bodied garden spider. Freddy grabbed an old broom that was leaning against the wall and poked the spider with the handle, eventually removing the massive spider from its web. It was at that very moment that, out of the corner of his eye, Freddy noticed a rather large hole in the partition that divided the two sheds, and he fancied for one second that he saw something poking through it. Freddy grinned wickedly and without hesitating he poked the broom handle with the spider clinging on the end through the hole in the partition, and heard a man's voice yell out loud, 'Ere what's goin' on!' Well Freddy ran out of the shed with his hand over his mouth laughing uncontrollably, his gang following behind him.

Five minutes later they all crept back again. It was very dark in there but fortunately there was just enough light for Freddy and his gang to see Winnie quite clearly. She was pressed up tight to the partition of the shed where the hole was, and her long grey skirt was hoisted up in the air. She wore no underwear at all—only her thick black stockings which were rolled over at the top. Her legs and everything else were exposed quite clearly for the boys to see! Winnie looked quite ridiculous with her cheek tightly pressed up to the partition, her hands were behind her back holding her skirts up, and she was rather ungraciously balancing herself on several upturned terracotta flower pots. But what was even more ridiculous was the sight through old Hancock's shed window. He, too, was thrust up against the partition of the shed. He was standing on a wooden seed tray, his flies were undone and he was leaning backward with his body thrust forward, but he still had his hat on, and he was muttering loudly: 'Winnie keep still for a moment my dear, try standing on a smaller flower pot, you're too high up for me to reach you. Aah that's better my dearest, I can feel you nicely now!' Then the boys heard Winnie making some strange moaning sounds and they couldn't believe their ears or their eyes.

Freddy and his gang were shaking like jellies trying to contain their laughter. They were convinced that the old wooden shed was rocking and would fall down at any moment, exposing the dirty old choir master sowing his seeds in Winnie the cobbler's wife, through the hole in the shed.

By the time Harold Hancock drove his pony and cart back home it was the evening and there was a full moon, and in the back of the cart was a huge bunch of rhubarb! Freddy and his gang were waiting for him behind the stone wall along Greenway Lane and they pelted old Hancock with old mangols, cow dung and clods of earth. 'That'll teach 'ee ya dirty old man,' shouted Freddy from behind the wall. He'd been dying to catch old Hancock out ever since Bessie Scott tipped the chamber pot over his best suit.

Old Hancock gave up his philandering ways for a little while; perhaps it was because he'd finished with Winnie. But a month later he was at 'it' again. It had been a beautiful hot June and the hay had been cut. Wealthy, old Farmer Rowlands was in his fields admiring his haystacks. There, amongst the freshly cut hay, was old Hancock rolling around with Elizabeth Wynne the clergyman's daughter, who was in her late thirties. That was it, the choir master's sins were exposed. From that day onwards Harold Hancock was banned from the church and eventually he, his wife and sixteen children moved away from the village.

RED DELICIOUS
Just Desserts

Rosie was one of the kindest, gentlest women you could ever meet. God had been generous by giving her a voluptuous, shapely body and enormous breasts. Yet, she was married to a very weatlhy, mean and cunning old miser; a 'money bags' who had his finger into every pie leaving Rosie hard up and poor. She was completely dominated by him, a victim of his emotional blackmail and his bullying. He called her 'fat, ugly and greedy' and other dreadful names, often ridiculing her in front of her friends.

The more money he made, and the more children she had by him, the worse he became. He would question and cross examine her if she was late back from shopping, interrogate her if she laughed and joked with another man, accusing her of having an affair with him. He was even jealous of the relationship she had with her mother, children and her friends. Many a time she wept and wanted to leave him, her children had grown up and didn't need her anymore, but her faith in God always stopped her from going, besides she had no money and nowhere to go.

The only bit of freedom that Rosie had (now that he had started following her to church) was her part-time nursing job in the local cottage hospital. Her patients were generally geriatrics, mostly dying and very ill men. The effect Rosie had on the old boys was quite amazing. At night, if they couldn't sleep, she would cradle them in her arms and sing them to sleep. Rosie had a lovely voice and several of the old men died contented and happy in her arms.

One of the lucky ones who did recover well enough to return home was old farmer Turner, but before he left he gave her a bit of helpful advice. 'Seeing your lovely big breasts Rosie, brought back a memory and reminded me of my old mother, who had a remedy for the cows when they got sore, hard udders.' He was silent for a moment, trying to remember the remedy. 'That's it, she used nipplewort the herb. I remember mother bruising the leaves of the herb and using it on her own breasts, when they were sore, as well as on her cows' teats. Could be a useful remedy Rosie for you one day, you never know.' And then he added cheekily, 'But I'd like to rub it on for you.'

Unfortunately Rosie's nursing job came to a sad end because the hospital closed and Rosie found herself stuck at home with her miserable husband. She didn't know what to do with herself until one of her daughters suggested she made puddings for a topless restaurant in London. So this is exactly what Rosie started to do. She loved cooking, and pudding making was a doddle—lots of cream and brandy was the secret.

But unbeknown to her husband Rosie also became a blues singer at the restaurant. The owner, notorious Nick, had heard Rose singing when she was delivering her tarts. He was so impressed with her voice that he offered her a job as the lunchtime singer. Rosie was stunned. She had never pictured herself as a professional singer. She enjoyed singing in the church choir and to the old boys in the

Rosie offered her admirers her big red juicy apples.

hospital, but she had never sung in public before. Nick took her into one of the dressing-rooms belonging to the topless waitresses and found Rosie a red satin basque with a plunging neckline to show off her bosoms, a pair of black fishnet tights and a saucy red garter decorated with a crimson rose. If any man dared touch or sniff the rose, Rosie would press a small rubber pump that was attached to the rose and it would squirt water in his face. On the table in the dressing-room was a big basket of beautiful rosy red delicious apples.

Nick offered Rosie a good wage to look 'Tarty but Tasteful'. Instead of handing out oranges like Nell Gwyn she would offer rosy-red apples to her audience. She was to be known as 'Rosie Red'.

Rosie was extremely nervous for her first appearance at lunchtime in 'Naughty Nicks', but Nick convinced her she could do it. He put his arms around her, kissed her and assured her she would be great and after a large gin and tonic and a gentle push on to the stage, Rosie Red sang. They were bluesy, romantic songs and she weaved her way in and out of the tables, pausing every now and then to hand out rosey-red apples, biting at an apple every now and then before she handed it over. Her performance caused a stir amongst the audience; they stood and clapped, they loved her. Rosie's reputation spread and people came from all over London to hear her sing.

The singing had put the life and sparkle back into Rosie's eyes. She also fell in love with Nick the night-club owner. With all his chunky chains and funny ways, he had a heart of gold. But she still couldn't bring herself to tell her husband she wanted to leave him. They had been together for a long time and she couldn't bear to hurt his feelings, even after what he had done to her.

But fate dictated the chain of events. Rosie's husband was invited by one of his clients to lunch at the club—a free business meal and a chance to hear Rosie Red sing. The audience clapped enthusiastically when Rosie appeared before them, weaving her curvaceous body in and out of the tables. You can imagine the look of horror on her husband's face when Rosie appeared dressed in her red basque and red feathered hat and slinky gloves. His mean eyes narrowed so you could hardly see them, he was horrified and full of rage. The row and fisticuffs that followed was dreadful. But eventually the bouncers jumped on the old miser and slung him out into the gutter.

With Nick by her side Rosie now had the strength and courage to leave her husband. She felt dreadful about breaking her wedding vows and spent an afternoon alone in the church, praying to God for forgiveness.

The next morning she had a letter from a solicitor explaining that old farmer Turner whom she had nursed at the cottage hospital had died and, for the kindness Rosie had bestowed upon him and other patients, he had left her several things including a beautiful gold crucifix that belonged to his mother. Rosie was overwhelmed by the gifts and she reckoned this was a sign of God's forgiveness—after all her husband had got his 'just desserts'.

ℋARVEST ℬREAD
The Fiddler's Fantasy

ack Jago was a Cornish pig farmer who liked a 'bit of crackling', and a fiddle on the side! For hundreds of years his family had been pig farmers, farming in the china clay area of Cornwall. But Jack was a bit different from his relatives, for he was a brilliant fiddle player and he often used to play his violin to his pigs, or porkers as he called them. Pigs are intelligent creatures and Jack reckoned that his pigs had an ear for music. They would snort and grunt affectionately around him when he played his fiddle.

He was indeed a brilliant violinist and played at garden fêtes, dances, churches and chapels all over Cornwall; he used to enjoy his tipple of drink that seemed to go with the job. One September Jack was invited to play his violin at the Harvest Festival in the local chapel. Unfortunately that day one of his pigs escaped from its pen and Jack was very late for the concert. By the time he had caught the pig, rushed home, had a bath and changed into his evening suit he had no time to eat his supper.

When he eventually arrived at the chapel the women's choir had already started

JACK WOULD LOVE TO GET HIS TEETH INTO HER.

singing, but the minister welcomed Jack with a large tumbler of 'Harvest Time Punch', and sat him down in the front pew to await his turn. Jack was starving and his stomach rumbled loudly. His mouth watered as he looked at the wonderful array of produce laid out on the snow-white table-cloth in front of him. But what caught his eye was the most splendid harvest bread that he had ever seen. It was golden brown and gilded with saffron and resembled a sheaf of corn. It took up nearly the whole length of the table and Jack couldn't take his eyes off it.

Jack was already feeling the effects of the punch. He had downed two glasses by the time the minister announced that it was time for him to play. Jack jumped up abruptly, his nose and cheeks were as red as the berries that decorated the church. He staggered up the aisles carrying his violin. Constance the pianist was already at the piano waiting for him to begin; she gave him a withering look as he stumbled up on the platform next to her. While he was playing something caught his eye and he looked sideways at the harvest bread—he thought he must be dreaming. There lay a voluptuous, naked nymphet, with the most wicked glint of lust in her eyes. Jack blinked and hesitated for a moment and the nymphet disappeared. He continued playing.

Jack played the violin that night better than he had ever done in his life before—Beethoven, Bach, gypsy music and Scott Joplin, all with a big grin on his face. Afterwards, Constance asked him why he grinned so much and he said, hiccuping loudly, 'Well I just kept looking at the harvest bread, and thinking how much I'd like to get my teeth into 'er.'

It was customary after the Harvest Festival to have a Harvest Supper in the village hall and auction off all the produce. Jack bid a lot of money for the harvest bread, determined to make it his own. He carried the enormous loaf home with him under his arm and later that evening, with a big smile on his face, he did get his teeth into it!

DUCKS AND DAFFODILS
A Tickle up the Tideford River

Dorothy (Dot) Bird and her young sister Maggie worked in the daffodil fields of the Tamar valley. It was back-breaking work picking the flowers and carrying the wicker baskets.

Dot was a very shy, naïve girl, in fact you could say she was a bit simple and she had never had a boyfriend before. But today she was excited for she was meeting Bertie Floyd and they were going for a walk down by the Tideford river. He was going to show her how to tickle a trout!

DOT WAS GOING TO HAVE A TICKLE UP THE TIDEFORD RIVER.

Bertie worked at the daffodil farm too and unlike Dot he wasn't a bit shy; in fact he was cock sure of himself, there was hardly a maid in the village he hadn't been out with. He was great fun to be with, a fine dancer and very popular with the girls, but he had smelly feet. Maggie had been out with Bertie before and warned Dot about Bertie's wandering hands and his dreadfully smelly feet. But Dot was too excited to care.

Bertie looked very handsome as he waited for Dot by the style near the river. He wore a green trilby hat, the brim pulled down seductively over his brown eyes. Dot's heart thumped as he took her hand while helping her over the style. As they walked down the narrow lane, overgrown with cow parsley, he put his arm around her waist holding her close and he told her how pretty she looked.

They passed the gamekeeper's cottage and he was in the garden with his springer spaniel; the young dog was charging up and down the garden chasing swallows. The gamekeeper called out to Bertie: 'Off to the river are we Bertie to "tickle trout"?' He winked at Bertie, and both men laughed. The springer spaniel followed them bounding through the long grass, leaping in the air chasing butter-flies. Bertie found a secluded spot by the river's edge and he laid his jacket on the grass and sat down. Dot timidly sat down beside him and suddenly he pounced on her, rolling her over and over, tickling her everywhere. Dot giggled uncontrollably and then she felt his strong fingers making their way up her skirts. Dot felt a bit nervous, he was so strong and persistent, but she managed to push him off. She reminded him that he promised to show her how to tickle trout. He was angry that she had put a stop to his love-making but he pulled his shoes and socks off and waded into the shallow water.

At that moment Dot got a massive whiff of his stinking feet—her sister was right! The pungent smell put her right off Bertie. Just then the young springer spaniel came bounding up and grabbed Bertie's smelly socks and ran off with them in his mouth. The smell disappeared. Bertie, unaware of what was going on, called out to Dot to join him. She pulled off her shoes and stockings, pulled her skirt up around her thighs and waded into the water. The shallow water was lovely and cooling around her feet. Bertie put his finger to his lips in a gesture of silence, bent slowly down and for a moment kept very still, with his hand in the water. Suddenly he flicked his wrist and there like magic was a wriggling trout tossed up in the air and on to the river bank.

Dot clapped her hands for she thought he was so clever, and she fancied him like mad. He must have sensed what lay behind the look in her eyes because he picked her up and carried her to the shore, kissing her as he carried her. Then he pushed her down on the grass next to the wriggling trout. Dot giggled and smiled because she had forgotten all about Bertie's smelly socks—she had better things on her mind. As they rolled around on the river bank, Dot squealing and laughing, the young springer spaniel ran off with the river trout in his mouth.

Dot married Bertie a year later. They had eleven children and lived happily ever after.

*L*OVE AMONG THE *B*UTTERCUPS
Cock and Bull story

*R*alph was a well respected farmer and head of the parish council. He lived on the outskirts of a village near St Austell, in an area known as the clay country, because of the huge pyramids of china clay that dominated the scenery. Most men worked in the clay pits, or as farm labourers, but if they were lucky like Ralph they owned their own farms. Cars were rarely seen and the only means of transport were bicycles, horses and pony and traps.

Ralph kept a fine herd of South Devon cows and a massive South Devon bull that he proudly exhibited in all the agricultural shows and he won several cups for the magnificent beast. It was funny the way Ralph resembled his bull with his thick-set body, big strong chest and his medium-length sandy-coloured hair, which like the bull's had a tendency to curl.

He was riding his old bay cob through the quiet lanes on the outskirts of the village. It was a glorious day in June and the Cornish hedgerows were full of pink campion, purple-coloured foxgloves and buttercups. A gentle breeze swayed the

BETTY WAS GOING TO HAVE A FROLIC WITH A FARMER.

ears of green corn which was scattered with red poppies. Large lambs frolicked in the fields and Ralph's prize bull lay in a buttercup field, contentedly chewing the cud with his cows. Suddenly a pony galloped down the narrow lane past him and, round the corner of the lane, Ralph came across Betty the baker's daughter. She was squealing and screaming hysterically. Her young pony had been startled by a stray sheep and it had bolted off, causing the trap to fall over on its side into the ditch, and Betty was caught in the wheels.

Anyway the baking-hot pasties had fallen on to Betty's face and all over her clothes as she lay helpless and frightened. She wasn't hurt but she couldn't move, because somehow the ribbons of her snow-white cotton drawers had tangled up in the spokes of the wheel. There she lay, her 'nose in the air', screaming and hollering for help and her legs splayed out in a very unladylike manner, showing off all her underwear. Ralph stared for a moment, then he jumped off his old mare to sort the distressed Betty out. He knew about Betty's reputation for being a snob and, as he removed his old knife from his pocket to cut her drawers free, he couldn't help laughing.

After he had untangled Betty he helped put the cart up the right way, but the wheels were damaged, and it was getting quite late. So he lifted Betty up on to the front of his horse and climbed up behind her. Ralph pulled himself up so close to Betty she could feel his breath on her face, and when he put his strong arms around her waist to hold the rains, her stomach flipped over. She had never been close to any man before, even her own father hadn't held her like this, and her body trembled.

Betty did become Ralph's lover, and they met every day after this, at the same time and the same place. If the weather was nice they made love in the corner of one of Ralph's fields, pleasantly overgrown with buttercups and cow parsley and near to where Ralph's prize bull grazed. If it was wet they met and made love in the hayloft of an old disused barn nearby. Nobody dared come in these fields because on the gate was a big sign in red paint saying 'BEWARE OF THE BULL' and another sign said 'TRESPASSERS WILL BE PROSECUTED'. So Ralph and Betty felt quite safe to do all their love-making there.

But village people don't miss much and what they don't see they make up, and 'tongues started wagging'. So the next day Sticky Hitchins and Itchy Morecombe, two trouble-makers, hid behind the stone wall in Ralph's field. Sure enough there was Ralph and Betty laid out in the long grass amongst the buttercups and cowparsley, nibbling bread and drinking cider. Presently Ralph threw himself upon Betty, tickling her so much that her straw hat fell off on to the grass. Then Ralph rolled her over and over, she laughed so much pleading with him to stop.

The boys started to laugh, but they couldn't see much so they stood up on the stone wall. Now they could see quite clearly Betty's black stockinged legs entwined around Ralph's strong body and her little buttoned boots pointing upwards. Then they saw something white flung up in the air. Assuming this to be her drawers the boys thought this was a good time for a bit of fun, so they crept through the long grass by the edge of the field where Ralph's prize bull was grazing, and undid the gate and waited.

The old South Devon bull ambled slowly into the field with his cows. At first he didn't notice the lovers, but then he heard a strange squealing sound, and out the corner of his eye he saw something bobbing up and down. The old bull was as gentle as a lamb with Ralph but he didn't recognize his master from behind! He stamped the ground and snorted and looked towards the mating pair. The boys were beside themselves with laughter, so much so that Sticky fell off the wall into the stinging nettles below.

Betty stuttered and screamed and Ralph ran round the field with only his shirt and socks on, with the bull chasing him; while Betty clambered up the stone wall, ripping her lovely white muslin dress on the brambles. She left behind Ralph's boots, his cap and her underclothes—and her lovely straw hat was eaten except for the feathers.

Shortly after this event Betty was packed off to London to stay with her aunt, to work as an apprentice seamstress. But that's not what the village folk thought, they had noticed that Betty was looking pale and plump, and another had seen her nibbling coal in the coal shed.

TITBIT

Betty used to pick baskets of the buttercups to take home with her. With the bright yellow flowers, picked on a sunny day, she would make a marvellous buttercup ointment.

A PINCH OF ROSEMARY
The Lusty Lord

Rosemary was the kitchen maid at the old manor house. She worked under the cook as her apprentice, and her duties included cooking the plainer dishes, the cakes and bread, and gathering and selecting vegetables, herbs and fruit.

At one time Rosemary's mother also worked at the manor house doing the same job, but she left rather abruptly under a cloud. Rosemary was born that same year! When she grew up she very much resembled the Lord of the Manor's daughter, with her black hair and her cornflower blue eyes. This gave rise to a lot of gossip amongst the village people.

Rosemary knew the Lord of the Manor had a reputation for chasing the women but so far she managed to escape his advances.

But today was her afternoon off and she was in love. She was meeting her boyfriend Tom the gardener. She popped on her best hat, the one with red poppies, and was just going out of the kitchen door when she remembered she had left a fruit cake in the oven.

A wonderful smell of spices and fruit filled the kitchen as she bent down to remove the cake from the big old oven. Suddenly she felt strong arms grabbing her around her tiny waist, almost lifting her off the floor. 'Tom you naughty . . .' she said dropping the cake on the floor. But she smelt the whiff of cigar smoke and brandy. It was the Lord of the Manor and he pushed Rosemary firmly and aggressively on to the cold flagstone floor, kissing her neck and running his icy cold fingers over her breasts, making her shiver and feel sick.

Suddenly there was a loud quacking and all the young ducklings who had been kept in the backyard, marched boldly into the kitchen. The Lord of the Manor must have left the back door open and the flock of hungry birds made a beeline towards the cake that Rosemary had dropped. Totally oblivious to the Lord of the Manor and what he was up to, they devoured the cake greedily. He was cross as he couldn't continue with his amorous advances with a mass of ducklings all round him, so he stood up, tidied his clothing and smoothed his hair. Just as he was leaving he pinched her roughly and waggling his finger at her he said, 'You naughty girl you shouldn't have left that door open, you could be dismissed for that. Now I will have to come and sort you out!' And he left by the back door with all the ducks following him.

ROSEMARY FELT STRONG HANDS AROUND HER TINY WAIST.

TITBIT

Rosemary is a good old-fashioned herb. At one time it was used at wedding ceremonies, for decorating churches and banqueting halls. Rosemary branches gilded and tied with colourful silk ribbons were given as a present to wedding guests as a symbol of Love and Loyalty—an old custom worth reviving. It grows in England better than anywhere else, bees love it and it is excellent used sparingly.

A FREE-RANGE HEN
The Postman's Pat

Johnny was the village postman and he had a great passion for amateur dramatics. In the evening, in the village hall, he and several other locals congregated to rehearse for the Christmas pantomime. It was while playing one of the ugly sisters in Cinderella that he met and fell for the Prince Charming. Her name was Patsy, a buxom, cheery woman with the best pair of legs that Johny had ever seen in his life.

Patsy was married to a butcher who owned a shop in the nearby town. He was a miserable, moody old man who bred poultry as a hobby—they were his pride and joy. His splendid black cockerel and hens were frequently supreme champions at the agricultural shows.

One morning, before Johnny went to work and when Patsy's husband was in the shop, she invited him in for a cup of tea. Patsy opened the front door wearing a revealing low-cut red spotted dress and nothing underneath it. It didn't take long for the two of them to start kissing and cuddling. Johnny's clothes were flung off at great speed and only his socks remained. Suddenly Patsy remembered that she had left the kettle on the stove. She rushed into the kitchen and, as she opened the door, all the steam from the kettle came drifting out like a cloud. But what came flying out through the steam was her husband's massive black labrador, barking loudly.

Meanwhile, Johnny, who was still standing stark naked except for his hand-knitted woollen socks, had made himself comfortable by the fireplace in a big armchair. It was the master's chair and the black labrador growled at Johnny menacingly. When Johnny tried to move, the large black creature bared its teeth in a snarl. Johnny, being a postman, didn't like dogs and he had given this one a smack over the nose with a newspaper more than once, so the dog didn't like Johnny either.

Johny called out frantically for Patsy to come and help him. She roared with laughter when she saw him sunk down in the chair naked except for his socks. But she couldn't move the dog or get close to Johnny. After an hour Johnny was getting cold and very worried for he had to be getting back to work. But the dog wasn't going to move. Patsy tried dangling a piece of fresh rabbit in front of the dog's nose, but nothing would budge him. In desperation Patsy rushed out into the garden and returned with her husband's favourite prize-winning black hen, hoping that the dog would chase it out of the house. But the dog still refused to move.

Patsy was getting anxious, what was she to do? In fact there was nothing she could do. So she phoned her husband at work and told him that Johnny was stuck in the armchair. In fear they both waited for the butcher to return. But as they heard him coming down the path the dog heard him too and, wagging his tail, he ran off leaving Johnny to make a quick getaway. He was so petrified he ran

PATSY RETURNED WITH ONE OF HER HUSBAND'S FREE-RANGE HENS.

through the kitchen, grabbing a tea-cloth, and out through the back door like a streak of lightning. He jumped the fence, ran down the lane and across the fields— stark naked except for the tea-cloth and those woolly socks.

$\mathscr{A}$CKNOWLEDGEMENTS

Great thanks go to Doreen who encouraged me to keep painting. To Keith Floyd who said my paintings contained 'Fresh and Fruity' ingredients like his recipes and that I should write a book, and to all the old folk who have 'been and gone'. Kathleen the cook, Arthur the horse breaker, Les the lamper, Caroline the house-keeper, Dick the builder, Roy the woodcutter, Mrs Hancock the vicar's maid, Mr Harris the market gardener, and Mary Kitchener my mother-in-law.

First published in Great Britain in 1993
by Boxtree Limited

Text © Carol Payne 1993
Illustrations © Carol Payne 1993

The right of Carol Payne to be identified as
Author of the Work has been asserted by her in accordance with the
Copyright, Designs and Patents Act 1988.

1 3 5 7 9 10 8 6 4 2

A · DELIAN · BOWER · Book
Conceived and edited by Delian Bower
18 Devonshire Place, Exeter EX4 6JA

Designed by Vic Giolitto
Typeset by Colin Bakké Typesetting, Exeter
Colour reproduction by Peninsula Repro Service, Exeter
Printed and bound in Hong Kong by Mandarin Offset International Limited

Boxtree Limited
Broadwall House
21 Broadwall
London SE1 9PL

A CIP catalogue entry for this book is available from the
British Library

ISBN 1 85283 503 6